Railways & Recollections 1959

Michael H. C. Baker

First published in 2017

British Library Cataloguing in Publication Data

A catalogue record for this book is available from the British Library.

ISBN 978 1 85794 496 9

Silver Link Publishing Ltd
The Trundle
Ringstead Road
Great Addington
Kettering
Northants NN14 4BW

Tel/Fax: 01536 330588
email: sales@nostalgiacollection.com
Website: www.nostalgiacollection.com

Printed and bound in the Czech Republic

Unless otherwise credited all the photographs were taken by the author or are from his collection.

Contents

Frontispiece: **YORK** A four-car Class 104 Birmingham RC&W diesel multiple unit sets out from York with a Harrogate service. Elsewhere in 1959 DMUs were operating more and more of the surviving branch-line passenger duties as well as on the main lines.

Introduction

1959 was the last year since early Victorian times when the production of steam locomotives for Britain's main-line railway system continued throughout the 12 months. Admittedly this consisted of a few of the last members of just one class, the 9F 2-10-0s. They were, however, among the finest ever built, and it was a combination of crass political incompetence and British Railways keeping its head firmly stuck in the sand that these locomotives had such a criminally short career. The very last BR steam locomotive, 9F 2-10-0 No 92220 *Evening Star*, was launched at a ceremony at Swindon Works on 18 March 1960, and all BR steam would be gone by the summer of 1968. Admittedly, steam was abolished with equally unseemly haste elsewhere, notably in the USA, and in many countries such as France, Germany and, eventually, China steam locomotives were broken up well before reaching their allotted span. After *Evening Star* there would be no more, at least until we entered the era of full-scale replicas with the LNER-designed 'A1' 'Pacific' No 60163 *Tornado* in 2008.

It has to be said that, whatever enthusiasts felt about the impending doom of the steam locomotive, the travelling public, while they may have had a lingering affection for the romantic side of this form of power, were certainly not in love with the dirt, pollution, noise and general air of belonging to the past that it epitomised. Much of the population was more

SOUTHALL A 9F and a GWR '61xx' 2-6-2T at Southall depot. The 9Fs worked all over England, Wales and Scotland during their short lifespan, although were largely absent from the Southern Region, where passenger traffic was the big money-spinner.

SWINDON Overhauled Collett 0-4-2T No 1466 is coupled to a newly built 9F 2-10-0 at Swindon Works. By chance the 0-4-2T would be preserved, the very first locomotive to be acquired by the four Southall schoolboys who were founder members of the Great Western Society.

affluent than ever before. They could afford to travel. They were in the mood for something clean, was more swift and up-to-date. Successful transatlantic commercial travel had begun with the Boeing 707 the previous year. In October 1959 Harold Macmillan won the general election for the Conservatives with the slogan, 'You've never had it so good.' He had a majority of 100 over Labour, and the Liberals had six MPs.

I met Macmillan, in a manner of speaking,

when working as a carriage-cleaner and porter at King's Cross station (described later). One August afternoon I was standing on Platform 5, minding my own business and waiting to polish the door handles of an express that had just arrived from Edinburgh, when a group of important-looking gentlemen came towards me, ushering other passengers aside. In the centre of the group was the Prime Minister, who had been summoned from an appointment on the grouse moor to an emergency cabinet

meeting. One of the new MPs to take her seat that October was Margaret Thatcher.

The Queen (the magazine, not Her Majesty – I did a double-take when I came across this quote) declared that 'Britain has launched into an age of unparalleled lavish living.' Unemployment was 2%, and the average standard of living between 1950 and 1965 went up by 40%. Unskilled and semi-skilled workers in particular saw their conditions, and ambitions, rise markedly. However, if by 1959 Britain was one of 'the most affluent countries in the world', it still lagged behind the members of the European Common Market, who had more TV sets, washing machines, and freezers per head of their populations.

'A new television set is delivered.'

The arrival of the Morris Mini Minor.

On 26 August the British Motor Corporation launched the Morris Mini – the mini skirt came a little later. Nevertheless, the Mini's predecessor, the Morris Minor, very much a car of the late 1940s and early '50s, remained a favourite with more conservative drivers into the 1960s, and together with the Ford Popular outsold all other small family cars.

In 1958 Harry Webb had changed his name

The author's father, Leonard, with a Morris Minor and Ford Popular.

to Cliff Richard, and in 1959 had his first No 1 single. Adam Faith also had his first chart-topper in that year, the pair rivalling in popularity Elvis Presley, the Everly Brothers, Roy Orbison and the like from across the Atlantic. When Buddy Holly, together with the Big Bopper and Richie Valens, was killed in an air crash on 3 February 1959 it made headline news on the BBC.

Meanwhile John Lennon and Paul McCartney had already met with George Harrison and were beginning to make a name for themselves on Merseyside, although this did not prevent Lennon, to my certain knowledge, from once being booed off the stage at an art school hop in the college in Hope Street.

The western world, and the UK in particular, was on the cusp of the Swinging Sixties.

SHREWSBURY Although in decline, the freight business, vastly less glamorous but enormously important to the railways, was still largely in the hands of steam, and coal was still profitable and a very significant money-earner. A GWR '28xx' Class 2-8-0 approaches Shrewsbury from South Wales with a goods train, most of the vehicles in view being ancient, wooden-bodied coal wagons, which, without continuous brakes, could not safely be run much above 30mph. A pannier tank is shunting in the bottom left of the picture, and over on the right is the former LMS Shrewsbury depot at Coleham, with the GWR shed immediately behind it.

SHREWSBURY Three elderly LNWR-built 'G2a' 0-8-0s are in store at Coleham depot, Shrewsbury. All would steam again, briefly, the last of the class being withdrawn in 1962 One, No 49395, has been preserved.

It was an odd thing about the British 0-8-0. None of the southern companies would have anything to do with it. The SECR, LB&SCR and LSWR never had much need for big freight engines and the GWR went in for the 2-8-0. But elsewhere it was very popular. The Midland Railway had a daft aversion to anything big and powerful for either freight or passenger work, even though it built a handful of excellent 2-8-0s for the Somerset & Dorset Joint Railway, and when Fowler did built 0-8-0s for the LMS they weren't a patch on the vast army of LNWR 0-8-0s that they were supposed to supersede.

BRISTOL Unloading goods on the quayside at M Shed, Bristol Docks
Although this could easily be a scene from the late 1950s, it is actually a
reconstruction staged in October 2016. Like many large docks, Bristol still
boasted an extensive railway system into the 1960s. Most have entirely
disappeared but a small section of that at Bristol survives, over which steam
regularly operates a passenger service.

Right: A timetable for the railbuses taking over from steam on the
Cirencester and Tetbury branches in June 1959. Unfortunately they were not
able to ensure the lines' survival – both closed on 4 April 1964.

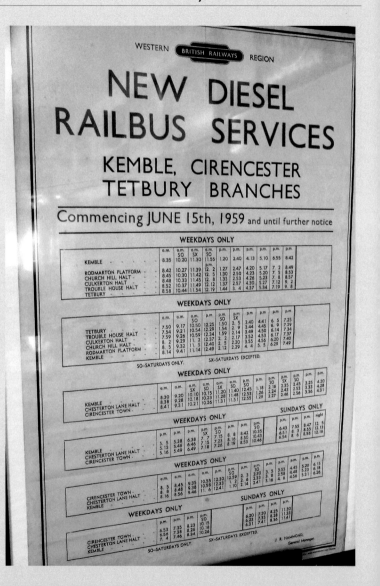

DOVEY JUNCTION A four-car Metro-Cammell DMU waits for a BR Standard Class 4MT 4-6-0 to arrive and clear the single-line section. The Metro-Cammell units were among the longest-lived of the first-generation DMUs, proving an excellent investment.

Old Oak Common

WEST CROYDON Two of my favourite haunts in steam days, and later, were around Subway Junction, on the approach to Paddington, and Old Oak Common, a little further out. To get there from my home in Thornton Heath I would usually take the 630 trolleybus, the longest regular trolley route in London, which terminated a couple of stops further on at the curiously, if accurately, named 'Near Willesden Junction'. Sitting beside the tracks at Old Oak Common, which one

reached down an ungated slope and to which no railwayman ever seemed to object, one could clearly detect the distinctive hoot of a Stanier whistle, as a 'Princess Royal', 'Princess Coronation' or 'Royal Scot' sped through Willesden Junction a mile away.

1959 Happenings (1)

January
- Tyne Tees Television goes on air in the North East of England
- The USSR successfully launches Luna 1 moon probe
- Rebel troops led by Che Guevara enter city of Havana, followed shortly by Fidel Castro
- Charles De Gaulle inaugurated as first president of French Fifth republic
- Motown Records founded by Berry Gordy Jnr

February
- UK grants Cyprus its independence
- Prime Minister Harold Macmillan holds talks with Soviet leader Nikita Khrushchev in USSR
- First successful test firing of Titan intercontinental ballistic missile from Cape Canaveral, Florida
- Fidel Castro becomes Premier of Cuba

March
- Large CND demonstration in Trafalgar Square
- Archbishop Makarios returns to Cyprus from exile
- Dalai Lama flees Tibet and is granted asylum in India
- Debut of the Barbie doll

April
- Official name of administrative county Hampshire changed from 'County of Southampton' to 'County of Hampshire'
- United Dairies merges with Cow & Gate to form Unigate Dairies
- Icelandic gunboat fires on British trawlers in first of 'Cod Wars'
- St Lawrence Seaway opens, linking Great Lakes with Atlantic Ocean

Above: **SUBWAY JUNCTION** The fastest train in the UK, 'The Bristolian', was still steam-hauled at the beginning of 1959, but would go over to diesels in June. On 3 June, four days before steam haulage ended, 'Castle' Class No 5085 *Evesham Abbey* glides through the junction on the approach to Paddington with the up service. The seven-coach train consists of six BR Mark I carriages and one GWR-designed 12-wheel dining car. *Evesham Abbey* was originally a 'Star' Class locomotive, built in 1922 and rebuilt as a 'Castle' in 1939, and although it was not defined by the GWR as a rebuild it certainly would have been on other railways. It says something about the quality of Swindon designs that what was essentially a 37-year-old

locomotive could be put in charge of the UK's fastest train. *Evesham Abbey* was eventually withdrawn in February 1964.

Right: **SUBWAY JUNCTION** The mixed-traffic 'Grange' 4-6-0s were relatively rare in the London area, but one regular working, certainly in the summer of 1959, was the 7.30pm Paddington to Oxford and Wolverhampton. No 6866 *Morfa Grange* is in charge of a complete train of GWR-built carriages on 3 June. In the foreground are the Underground tracks of the District's Hammersmith line.

OLD OAK COMMON The GWR's finest and most powerful passenger locomotives were the 30 members of the 'King' Class, dating from 1927-30. Most famous of them all, and now preserved as part of the National Collection, is No 6000 *King George V*, seen here simmering away majestically at Old Oak Common, the largest depot on the Western Region. On his buffer beam he sports the bell with which he was presented during a triumphal visit to the United States in 1927.

SUBWAY JUNCTION Commuter traffic in and out of Paddington was not as heavy as that at many other London termini. It was mostly in the capable hands of the 70 '61xx' 2-6-2Ts, dating from 1931, and would remain so until DMUs took over in 1960/61. Here No 6164 speeds past Subway Junction with a down train of five Hawksworth non-corridor carriages. Many of these final examples of Swindon-designed, plain but comfortable vehicles entered service in the early Nationalisation years.

OLD OAK COMMON The 'County' Class 4-6-0s, the first of which appeared in 1945, were initially declared by the GWR's publicity department to be the two-cylinder equivalent of the four-cylinder 'Castles'. In their original condition they hardly lived up to this billing, but once fitted with double chimneys, and the rather conservative Western drivers had come to terms with how best to handle them, they proved an excellent investment and were much appreciated on the heavily graded routes in Cornwall and along the North to West main line. By 1959 they were relatively rare visitors to London, but here No 1017 *County of Hereford*, almost certainly just out of Swindon Works after overhaul and looking very fetching, is passing Old Oak Common in charge of a 12-coach up Cheltenham Spa express, the first four carriages of which are of GWR origin, the rest BR Mark 1s. Another late Collett carriage, still in red and cream livery, can be seen on the empty carriage road. A workman, in standard attire, complete with flat cap, hardly changed in 30 or more years, is walking towards Old Oak Common depot in the far distance. The overhead wires for the 630 trolleys can be seen on the impressive bridge carrying Scrubs Lane over the tracks (I'm afraid that's the best we can do – I never did manage to get a trolleybus in the same picture as a train). By 1959 London's trolleybus network, once the largest in the world, was beginning to be dismantled, and would be gone by late 1962.

OLD OAK COMMON Across from Old Oak Common steam depot were the carriage sidings, now the home of HSTs, and here we see the GWR's answer to the Pullman. This was one of the very grand Ocean Saloons, built in the early 1930s for the boat train traffic at Plymouth. If you were in a great hurry to get from New York to London in liner days a quicker route than landing at Southampton was to do so at Plymouth, especially if you travelled in the French Line's *Normandie*, which for a time in the 1930s held the Blue Riband for the fastest Atlantic crossing. These saloons never lost their chocolate and cream livery, and most have been preserved;

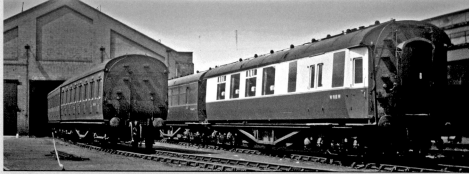

I was lucky enough to make several trips on the main line in this particular example as part of the Great Western Society's vintage train, which ran in the early 1970s. On the next track is a Churchward non-corridor First of about 1920, used on suburban services out of Paddington.

Southern steam

SELSDON Brighton-based British Railways Standard 2-6-4T No 80152, built at Brighton, has no difficulty with its train of four Maunsell corridors of c1930 vintage as it climbs towards Selsdon station with a Tunbridge Wells West train.

NORWOOD JUNCTION The only steam seen regularly passing Thornton Heath was on the Oxted line passenger and freight trains. BR Standard tanks worked most Oxted line passenger trains with great efficiency, and were usually kept pretty clean, especially those shedded at Tunbridge Wells; well, they hadn't got much choice if they chose to reside in spa town, not wanting any complaints from 'disgusted' residents! Much of the freight traffic was powered by elderly 0-6-2Ts and 0-6-0s of LB&SCR origin, which were shedded within cycling distance of home at Norwood. However, as no passenger, and certainly no named engines, lived there, I seldom bothered to visit — much to my later regret. In store at the shed are two LB&SCR freight locomotives. Nearest the camera is 'C2X' No 32543, next to 'E5' 0-6-2T No 32413. Beyond is a very shiny former SE&CR 'birdcage' carriage, which must have been newly adapted for departmental use. Both locomotives would steam again.

Right: **VAUXHALL** 'Lord Nelson' No 30853 *Sir Richard Grenville* gets to grips withy of a down Ocean Liner express bound for Southampton Docks as it accelerates through Vauxhall.

Below: **REDHILL** On the far left is an LSWR-designed '0700' 0-6-0, which will be heading off to Guildford and, perhaps, Reading. A 2HAL EMU is bringing up the rear of a London-bound service in the centre, and nearest the camera is a London Bridge to Brighton stopping train headed by a 4LAV.

Below: **SOUTHAMPTON** At this time boat train traffic was a significant feature of the Waterloo to Southampton line. A BR Standard Class 4MT is in charge of a short freight at Southampton Central with the most famous of all the transatlantic liners of this period, the RMS *Queen Mary*, alongside the Western Docks in the background. *Queen Mary* would make her last voyage out of Southampton in 1967, to become a floating museum in California.

SALISBURY 'Schools' Class 4-4-0 No 30912 *Downside* departs from Salisbury with a train for Portsmouth Harbour, consisting of a former LNER Full Brake and an early Bulleid corridor set.

July
 UK postcodes first introduced, experimentally in
  Norwich
 Mental Health Act, modernising care of mental
  disorders, and Obscene Publications
  Act become law
 At opening of American National Exhibition in
  Moscow, US Vice President Richard Nixon
  and USSR Premier Nikita Khrushchev engage
  in 'Kitchen Debate'

August
 Barclays becomes first bank to install a computer
 House of Fraser acquires Harrods for £37
  million
 First Mini goes on sale
 PM Harold Macmillan and US President
  Eisenhower make joint TV broadcast from
  Downing Street
 US spacecraft Explorer 6 sends first picture of
  Earth from orbit
 Hawaii is admitted as 50th US state

September
 USSR's Luna 2 becomes first man-made object
  to crash on Moon
 USSR Premier Nikita Khrushchev and his wife
  tour US at invitation of President
  Eisenhower
 Xerox 914, first plain paper copier, introduced to
  public
 First official large unit action of Vietnam War
  takes place, when US troops are ambushed
  by Vietcong force

SALISBURY A class of locomotive that had been a mainstay of services between Waterloo, the Dorset coast and the West Country for decades was the 'N15' 'King Arthurs', which had originated on the LSWR. The last of the original examples was withdrawn in 1957, and 1959 would see 17 of the Southern Railway-built locos taken out of service with the inauguration of the first stage of that year's Kent Coast electrification. I had a soft spot for the 'King Arthurs' – they seemed the epitome of the Southern Railway express locomotive between the wars, even though, with their windowless cabs, a trifle dated compared to the 'Lord Nelsons' and the 'Schools'. Here at Salisbury shed are, from left to right, one of the earliest Southern Railway 'King Arthurs', No 30449 *Sir Torre*, one of the 'Scotch Arthurs', North British-built No 30774 *Sir Gaheris*, GWR-built Collett 'Mogul' No 7332 and, just visible, part of the cab and tender of a GWR 'County' Class 4-6-0. *Sir Torre* was withdrawn in December 1959 and *Sir Gaheris* a month later.

End of steam to the Kent coast

15 June 1959 was the day when the first stage of a two-part conversion of the lines between London and the Kent Coast from steam to electricity would take place. Already diesel locomotives had begun to appear, mostly shunters, but also a few on the main line to the Kent Coast centred on Ramsgate. The occasion warranted the stretching of my student grant to a return ticket from East Croydon to Ramsgate on the Saturday before, 13 June, which would be the last day of regular steam operation. Was ever public money better spent?

Once, long, long ago, all trains from London to the Kent Coast shared the main Brighton line as far as Redhill, where they swung eastwards and pursued an almost straight line through Tonbridge to Ashford. In the 1920s and early '30s this was a great boon to airline pilots heading from Croydon, which was then London's premier airport, to the continent, as they could lean out of their open cockpits and descend low enough not just to follow the railway line, but also check the names of Tonbridge and Ashford stations, which had been thoughtfully painted on their roofs. Mind you, who but mad adventurers would want to travel in such uncomfortable and often dangerous conditions – sometimes high winds would prevent take-off or bring about forced landings, sometime with fatal results – when one could luxuriate in a Pullman, not just on the 'Golden Arrow' but in many of the Folkestone, Dover and Ramsgate expresses?

The original Redhill route had long become redundant for trains to the Kent Coast, but just one through train survived, the 4.50am from London Bridge (it actually commenced at Holborn Viaduct, but this was not shown in the public timetable) to Ramsgate. Motive power was usually a member of that finest of all 4-4-0s, R. E. L. Maunsell's 'Schools' Class. It was all too easy to regard the 'Schools' as simply another top-link express engine, the equal of a 'King Arthur' or 'Lord Nelson', or even, in certain respects, a Bulleid 'light Pacific', and forget that it was a 4-4-0, a wheel arrangement that was supposed to have been superseded back at the beginning of the century by 'Atlantics', 4-6-0s and, eventually, 'Pacifics'.

So it was that No 30926 *Repton* pulled into East Croydon on what was already a bright, cloudless day, and warming up nicely. I ensconced myself, not in a Pullman, but in a perfectly acceptable narrow-bodied Maunsell corridor compartment. It was part of a three-coach set dating from the late 1920s that had spent practically all its career on the Hastings line, but now that DEMUs had taken over there it was serving out its time elsewhere. I had the compartment to myself for the whole journey; it was, after all, almost the longest day of the year, so who but a steam enthusiast would want to be up before 5am when there would be another 17 hours of daylight?

TONBRIDGE 'H' Class 0-4-4T No 31533 is in charge of a pair of former LB&SCR and SER carriages forming a Maidstone West train.

ASHFORD Here we see my train leaving Ashford. *Repton* is still with us, one of the three preserved members of the 'Schools' Class.

Right: **ASHFORD** After 1959 the new diesels were increasingly prevalent. In 1960 the Birmingham/Sulzer Type 3s (later Class 33) were introduced and a brand new example is in charge of a train of coast-bound Bulleid corridors as an 'N' Class 2-6-0 approaches with a long London-bound freight, many of the wagons containing coal from one of the four Kent Coast collieries still working in 1959.

Below right: **RAMSGATE** At Ramsgate 'Schools' 4-4-0s were still in charge of expresses from London, and No 30919 *Harrow* is seen pulling out with the empty stock of the 11.30am from Victoria. All around are rakes of 4CEP and 4BEP express EMUs, parked on every available siding in the Ramsgate area, ready to take up work the following Monday, by which time, of course, they would have almost a monopoly and steam would be all but banished.

A postcard sent from Ramsgate in 1959.

1959 Arrivals & Departures

Arrivals

Sade (Helen Folasade Adu)

	Singer	16 January
Linda Blair	Actress	22 January
Vic Reeves	Comedian and actor	24 January
Lol Tolhurst	Musician (The Cure)	3 February
Renée Fleming	American soprano	14 February
John McEnroe	Tennis player	16 February
Nick Griffin	Politician, BNP	1 March
Steve McFadden	*EastEnders* actor	20 March
David Hyde Pierce	Actor (*Frasier*)	3 April
Emma Thompson	Actress and screenwriter	15 April
Sean Bean	Actor	17 April
Robert Smith	Musician (The Cure)	21 April
Paula Yates	TV presenter	24 April
Sheena Easton	Singer	27 April
Ben Elton	Comedian and writer	3 May
Ian McCulloch	Musician	5 May
Paul Whitehouse	Comedian	17 May
(Stephen) Morrissey	Musician	22 May
Bob Mortimer	Comedian	23 May
Rupert Everett	Actor	29 May
Martin Brundle	Motor racing driver/commentator	1 June
Hugh Laurie	Actor and musician	11 June
Sophie Grigson	Cookery writer and chef	19 June
Julie Birchill	Journalist	3 July
Jim Kerr	Musician (Simple Minds)	9 July
Kevin Spacey	Actor and director	26 July
Jeanette Winterson	Novelist	27 August
Morten Harket	Singer (A-Ha)	14 September
Greg Proops	Comedian	3 October
Simon Cowell	Music producer	7 October
Kirsty MacColl	Singer/songwriter	10 October
Marie Osmond	Singer	13 October
Sarah Ferguson	Duchess of York	15 October
Gary Kemp	Musician and actor	16 October
Niamh Cusack	Actress	20 October

Peter Mullan	Actor	2 November
Bryan Adams	Singer	5 November
Paul McGann	Actor	14 November
Charles Kennedy	Politician	25 November
Lorraine Kelly	Presenter and journalist	30 November
Gwyneth Strong	Actress	2 December
Jasper Conran	Fashion designer	12 December
Andy McNab	Soldier and novelist	28 December
Tracey Ullman	Comedian, actress and writer	30 December
Val Kilmer	Actor	31 December

Departures

Cecil B. DeMille	Film director (b1881)	21 January
Mike Hawthorn	Racing driver (b1929)	22 January
The Big Bopper (J. P. Richardson)	Musician (b1930)	3 February
Buddy Holly	Musician (b1936)	3 February
Ritchie Valens	Musician (b1941)	3 February
Lou Costello	Actor and comedian (b1906)	3 March
Raymond Chandler	Novelist (b1888)	26 March
Frank Lloyd Wright	Architect (b1867)	9 April
John Foster Dulles	US politician (b1888)	24 May
Charles Vidor	Film director (b1900)	4 June
Ethel Barrymore	Actress (b1879)	18 June
Billie Holiday	Singer (b1915)	17 July
Jacob Epstein	Sculptor (b1880)	19 August
Bohuslav Martinu	Czech composer (b1890)	28 August
Gerard Hoffnung	Humorist (b1925)	25 September
Errol Flynn	Actor (b1909)	14 October
Heitor Villa-Lobos	Brazilian composer (b1887)	17 November
Stanley Spencer	Painter (b1891)	14 December

RAMSGATE Long-withdrawn 'D' Cla[ss] 4-4-0 No 31501 serves as a stationary boiler at Ramsgate depot.

Right: **RAMSGATE** One of the more remarkable sights that day was one of the elderly but long-lived and highly efficient 'H' Class 0-4-4Ts of the South Eastern & Chatham Railway, No 31326, in charge of an inter-regional express, the 9.18am Margate to Birkenhead, and this despite a number of modern BR Standard Class 3 2-6-2Ts being available.

Above: **RAMSGATE** Bulleid 'Pacifics' were, of course, much in evidence on Ramsgate shed, but so also were tender engines from earlier generations, 'N' Class 2-6-0s, and at least one 'King Arthur', No 30802 *Sir Durnore*, as well as those wonderful rebuilt 'D1' and 'E1' 4-4-0s dating from SE&CR days.

Southern electrics

Below: **VICTORIA** 4SUB No 4501 stands alongside a 4COR. The latter was built in the late 1930s for the express services to Portsmouth and Bognor and will shortly be setting off via the Mid-Sussex line for the Sussex resort. The 4SUB is one of the very last wooden-bodied suburban units; the two coaches nearest the barrier are of LSWR origin, the rear two ex-LB&SCR, the unit having been reformed a few years earlier in the mid-1950s.

SOUTH CROYDON Being brought up in Thornton Heath, a somewhat undistinguished suburb of Croydon – its best-known former inhabitant being Dick Turpin's auntie – there was nothing novel about electric trains, which had been around since my father was a boy, although he could also recall yellow-painted Stroudley engines. Wooden-bodied EMUs of pre-Grouping origin, converted from steam stock by the Southern Railway, had been standard fare, but by 1959 most had been replaced by Bulleid all-steel units or their very similar BR standard successors; when they first appeared immediately after the war struck me as being ultra-modern, if not particularly comfortable. Here a Bulleid all-steel EMU on a Victoria to Coulsdon North working approaches South Croydon, with a 4COR express unit in the distance.

Right: **GATWICK AIRPORT** Semi-fast and fast units were of Southern Railway origin. The six-carriage PULs and PANs that operated the Sussex Coast express services looked impressive, especially the Pullman cars incorporated in the PUL units, but their riding qualities left a good deal to be desired, as did the three all-Pullman five-car units that worked the 'Brighton Belle'. My first, eagerly anticipated ride in the massive, deep-seated cushions of a 6PUL motor car was something of a disappointment, for it thumped and shuddered all the way from East Croydon to Lewes.

Below: **HASSOCKS** The up 'Brighton Belle', consisting of two 5BEL Pullman units, speeds through Hassocks with the South Downs in the background. I always felt that the semi-fast 4LAV and 2BIL units rode rather better, although the later Bulleid HALs were horrible. I travelled in the 'Brighton Belle' a couple of times, once in the driver's cab, and very primitive it seemed by comparison with today's electric trains, but it could certainly deliver the goods, or rather the passengers, among them a clutch of theatrical celebrities who, not surprisingly, took up residence in some very upmarket and supremely elegant Regency accommodation in Brighton and Hove.

Regular Pullman patrons soon learned not to attempt to sip their tea or coffee at certain locations, the junction of the Eastbourne and Brighton lines at Keymer Junction being particularly notorious. Here a 6PAN express unit waits in the sidings at Gatwick Airport as a Viscount turboprop airliner approaches the runway. A post-war 2HAL unit, reserved for air passengers, waits in the far sidings to be attached to a train from the Mid-Sussex line to return to Victoria.

1959 Happenings (3)

October

- 300 people rescued from fire on Southend Pier
- UK General Election results in record third successive Conservative victory, with increased majority of 100 seats; one of new MPs is Margaret Thatcher
- Ronnie Scott's Jazz Club opens in Soho
- US TV anthology series *The Twilight Zone* premieres on CBS
- USSR probe Luna 3 sends back first ever photos of far side of the Moon
- First appearance of cartoon character Astérix the Gaul
- The Aberfan colliery disaster kills 116 children and 28 adults.

*

- British spy George Blake escapes from Wormwood Scrubs prison.
- Spain closes its Gibraltar border to non-pedestrian traffic.
- Barbados is granted independence.

November

- First section of M1 motorway, and M45 and M10 spurs, opened between Watford and Crick, near Rugby, following ceremony near Toddington by Minister of Transport Ernest Marples
- London Transport introduces production Routemaster buses into public service
- Prestwick and Renfrew become first UK airports with duty-free shops
- Britain becomes founder member of European Free Trade Association
- MGM epic *Ben-Hur* is released and becomes studio's greatest hit so far, later winning a record 11 Academy Awards

The Bluebell Railway

HORSTED KEYNES 15 March 1959 saw what many would regard as the beginning of the preservation movement when a group met to attempt to buy the line from East Grinstead to Culver Junction, north of Lewes, from BR. It quickly became clear that this was too ambitious, so the group concentrated on the section between Horsted Keynes and Sheffield Park, and thus the Bluebell Railway was born, trains beginning to run in 1960.

In the very early days the railway painted its motive power and carriages in a blue livery and even named one of its first acquisitions, a former SE&CR 'P' Class 0-6-0T, *Bluebell*. It is seen here arriving at a very overgrown Horsted Keynes station hauling two former SE&CR non-corridor carriages, with a former Great Northern Railway saloon and another SE&CR carriage in the siding.

Diesel-electric units on the Southern

In 1959 steam was far less in evidence on suburban traffic in the London area than it had once been, particularly south of the Thames, where electrification had long been dominant. Dieselisation was also beginning to make itself felt, and one group of lines that saw steam largely replaced by diesel units, beginning in November 1957, was that serving the Portsmouth, Southampton, Salisbury, Winchester and Andover area.

Looking back to January 1959, *The Railway Observer* noted that 'the area … has never enjoyed such a frequent service … and that in the first complete year of operation there is an increase in revenue on all lines served.' This was hardly surprising if more trains were running, but nevertheless 'the diesel trains were well received by the general public.' Actually they were diesel-electric, the intention being that they might one day be quite easily adapted to become straight electrics. This never happened and throughout their careers they were handicapped, in comparison with a straight DMU, by virtually half of one carriage being occupied by the traction motors. One of the great advantages of a diesel unit over a locomotive-hauled train, and one that had great appeal for both passengers and enthusiasts, was that one could see ahead or behind, opening up vistas never before possible. Not so with a diesel-electric unit.

The Railway Observer further commented that 'rough riding of the motor coaches has been [a] complaint … but this is being overcome.' But it never really was. I travelled a lot on these units and the later but similar Oxted line examples. They did not ride as well as the steam-hauled stock they replaced, and were certainly nothing like as spacious and comfortable as the best of the rakes of Bulleid corridor carriages. As for style, this was a concept alien to them. Just like the long-vanished LB&SCR electrics, the more or less flat ends of the driving coaches simply had windows cut into them. One was left with the strong impression that the designers, if indeed there were any, had simply said, 'There it is, job done, take it or leave it.' But they were efficient, were more frequent and enabled some of the lines on which they appeared to stay open, but by no means all.

EAST CROYDON A 'Hampshire' DEMU arrives with an up Oxted line service in somewhat wintry conditions.

One such line, 'saved' by the DEMUs, was the Winchester to Alton branch. *The Railway Observer* declared that 'some staff said the [units] would never pay. This has been proved wrong and the service is becoming very popular as an alternative route to London.' But not popular enough. The line closed in 1973, and although in the preservation era the Watercress Line reopened much of the route and once again Bulleid 'Pacifics', *Lord Nelson* himself, 'S15s' and Maunsell 2-6-0s returned to their old stamping ground, this did not include

the section between Winchester and Alresford, and thus the alternative through route from London to the Hampshire coast was lost for good.

I often visit the Swindon & Cricklade Railway and was somewhat taken aback a few years ago to find awaiting me at Blunsdon station none other than an SR DEMU. Now this would certainly not have been very high on my list of preservation must-haves, but the Cricklade people obviously loved it. They were distraught when one of the carriages was destroyed by vandals early in 2016 but, most surprisingly and certainly teaching me a lesson, was how not only the preservation world but also the local community rallied round, provided support, both physical and financial, and in the not too distant future the old 'growler' will once again be growling through Wiltshire.

HURST GREEN JUNCTION A later version was built for the non-electrified routes in Surrey, Sussex and Kent, chiefly the Oxted line. The leading vehicles had fibreglass cab fronts which very slightly improved their appearance. Seen here in 1969 three units, forming a Lingfield race special, pass the junction with the Tunbridge Wells West line, watched over by the LB&SCR-designed signal box. At this time one of the signals it controlled was one of the very last lower-quadrant LB&SCR examples still in use.

King's Cross

I had the good luck to be employed as a carriage-cleaner and porter in the summer of 1959 at King's Cross. Working there was excellent; not only was the job far from demanding, but from an enthusiast's point of view most long-distance trains were in the hands of 'Pacifics', and the East Coast route went in for 'Pacifics' in a greater variety than anywhere else on British Railways. Also the job paid well; tips for carrying passengers' luggage were a bonus, and overtime was plentiful. The foreman might say, 'Can you do a bit of extra this evening?' and I'd say, 'How much?' and he'd reply, 'If you can do two hours I'll clock you off for four,' and I would agree. The one unforgiveable sin, in between cleaning carriages and carrying luggage, was to be caught reading a book. Standing about looking vacant was fine.

In those days King's Cross was not especially appealing to the general public. Cubitt's handsome façade was obscured by various huts and additions and, once inside there was no concourse, so one found oneself almost within touching distance of locomotives, exuding steam, smoke and various odours, nectar to enthusiasts but something rather less welcome to the travelling public. There were areas that had long been neglected, where artefacts and unwanted detritus gave the impression of being untouched since LNER, possibly even GNR, days. I came across

a board, roughly sawn off, which, on being turned over, revealed the legend 'The Silver Ju'. One Saturday afternoon there was a train of Southern Region green-painted Maunsell carriages bound for Newcastle – God knows what it was doing at King's Cross! – with every toilet bereft of water. The only solution the foreman could provide was a packet of yellowing labels bearing the information 'Out of order L&NER'.

Students, even if they happened to be enthusiasts such as myself, were first and foremost doing the job for money. The previous summer I'd been a plumber's mate – no tips there. At King's Cross I struck up a friendship with Willy, studying medicine, a native of somewhere in West Africa. He was intending to buy a complete set of *Encyclopaedia Britannica*, which seemed to me a somewhat scattergun approach to acquiring knowledge, which would cost most of what he would earn over the summer, but he assured me he knew what he was doing.

My chief task was polishing the door and grab handles. These came in two varieties, those of LNER origin, and their BR successors. The latter were functional and stubby, the former more curvaceous and elegant. A far less pleasant job was the washing of carriage windows. This entailed standing in the 'four foot' between the carriages wielding a long-handled brush. This had a circular rubber seal which was supposed to prevent the water running down the handle and continuing into the operative's sleeve. Sometimes it did, sometimes it didn't. It was a job I usually

Gresley restaurant car among a rake of BR Mark 1s, illustrating the difference between the grab handles.

managed to avoid. A couple of times I was given the job of cleaning the windows of Copenhagen signal box, set in the deep cutting between the two tunnels on the approach to King's Cross. 'Make sure you walk over the top, through the potato depot – don't go through the tunnel,' warned the foreman sternly. But the temptation was too great and on the second occasion, making sure the foreman was ensconced in his hidey-hole between the main line and suburban sections of the station, I nipped smartly off the platform edge and slipped into the tunnel. The contrast with the bright sun outside and the stygian gloom inside was intense, but by keeping close – but not too close – to the gleaming rails I could see where I was going and headed towards the circle of light at the far end. Then the rails began to vibrate and I realised that a train had entered. Recesses were set at frequent intervals in the tunnel walls so I was safe enough. Nevertheless standing pressed against the smoke-blackened brickwork a matter of mere inches from a thundering, steam-wreathed 'A3' is not an experience anyone would be likely to forget

To clean the signal box windows I had to clamber out on to the narrow wooden footway, complete with bucket and leather, and keep a steady grip as the whole box shook every time a 'Pacific' pounded by. Never before or since have I been afforded such a close-up of the exhaust from a double-chimneyed racing machine. I was forcibly reminded of the fate of the gang of robbers in the classic Ealing comedy, *The Lady Killers*, who hid their loot in a house above the tunnels outside King's Cross

and, one by one, met a grisly end on the track beneath.

The signalman was a friendly chap, a cup of tea always ready, and only too happy to talk about his experiences. I could have spent much longer in an environment that was denied to all but a lucky few.

KING'S CROSS Until the much-needed 21st-century facelift King's Cross did not have much of a concourse and travellers entered more or less straight from the street to find themselves face-to-face with a towering 'Pacific', which was fine for the enthusiast but a bit overwhelming for others... Here are 'A1' No 60120 *Kittiwake*, which has arrived from Leeds, and 'A2/2' No 60502 *Earl Marischal*, which has brought in a Scandinavian boat train from Tyne Commissioners Quay. The LNER embraced the 'Pacific' with greater enthusiasm than any of the other 'Big Four' companies, and there were many variations on the theme. The Peppercorn-designed 'A1s' did not enter service until the very early days of British Railways and were considered excellent, powerful if somewhat rough-riding machines. The 'A2/2s' were rebuilds of Gresley's almost legendary 2-8-2s of 1934, which were intended to work between Edinburgh, Dundee and Aberdeen but, although immensely powerful, were not really suited to the tight curves encountered on this route and were rebuilt and brought south by Thompson, where they had a mixed reception.

Above: **KING'S CROSS** An 'A2' 'Pacific' departs with an express for the north.

Right: **KING'S CROSS** 'A3' No 60044 *Melton* is about to depart with the 'Yorkshire Pullman', with a supporting cast of cleaners and trainspotters.

Above: **KING'S CROSS** When I was working at King's Cross, each afternoon 'The Elizabethan' would arrive, dead on time, non-stop from Edinburgh Waverley, behind an immaculate 'A4' 'Pacific'. Here it is No 60027 *Merlin*; note that LNER Thompson-designed carriages, originally built for the 'Flying Scotsman' immediately after the war, are still preferred to BR standards.

1959 No 1 Records

January
Jane Morgan — *The Day The Rains Came*
Elvis Presley — *One Night/I Got Stung*

February
Shirley Bassey — *As I Love You*

March
Platters — *Smoke Gets In Your Eyes*
Russ Conway — *Side Saddle*

April
Buddy Holly — *It Doesn't Matter Anymore*

May
Elvis Presley — *A Fool Such As I/I Need Your Love Tonight*

June
Russ Conway — *Roulette*

July
Bobby Darin — *Dream Lover*
Cliff Richard and the Drifters — *Living Doll*

September
Craig Douglas — *Only Sixteen*

October
Jerry Keller — *Here Comes Summer*
Bobby Darin — *Mack the Knife*
Cliff Richard and the Shadows — *Travellin' Light*

December
Adam Faith — *What Do You Want*
Emile Ford and the Checkmates — *What Do You Want To Make Those Eyes At Me For?*

KING'S CROSS 'N2' 0-6-2T No 69592 is in charge of the empty stock of an up arrival. Such duties were a regular feature of the class's work in the London area and continued after Craven DMUs and Class 31 diesel-electric locomotives made deep inroads into steam on suburban work by late 1959. By the summer of 1960 there was only one regular steam-hauled suburban working, and by the end of 1962 the 'N2s' had all been withdrawn. Fortunately one of them, No 69523, has been preserved.

KING'S CROSS This view is from York Road suburban platform near the mouth of Gas Works Tunnel, looking back past a solitary trainspotter and the GNR signal box to the main arrival and departure platforms, where an 'A1' 'Pacific' and one of the long-lived Brush Type 2s (later Class 31) can be seen.

Above: **COPENHAGEN TUNNEL** 'A1' 'Pacific' No 60121 *Silurian* emerges from the tunnel and passes Copenhagen box with an up express.

Below: **WOOD GREEN** For 30 and more years most of the suburban services had been provided by some of the least comfortable carriages in regular use on the BR network. These were the Gresley-design sets of articulated 'Quad-arts', 97 sets in all, built between 1921 and 1929, which crammed in huge numbers of suburbanites and certainly got them to and from work in the City, although the shorter you were the less discomfort you had to put up with. At 6 feet I made sure I travelled in them only when essential and was always able to avoid the rush hour. In this scene at Wood Green, with a 'Quad-art' set in the background, 'K3' 2-6-0 No 61870 has a short goods; beyond is an 'L1' 2-6-4T, and just visible an 'N2'. The 'L1s' were handsome engines but never displaced either the 'N2s' or the GER-designed 'N7s', which also helped out on suburban services out of King's Cross.

WOOD GREEN 'N7' 0-6-2T No 69638 is on a down stopper but with a vastly superior class of train, a rake of five BR standard non-corridors. Being much more comfortable than the 'Quad-arts', they were popular with the customers, but less so with the operating authorities, who kept them away from the heaviest rush-hour workings. There were 134 'N7s', built between 1914 and 1927. Withdrawal began in 1957, with 41 going in 1959; the class became extinct, except for one preserved example, in 1962.

Liverpool Street

Electrification was planned for the King's Cross suburban services, but at Liverpool Street the changeover from steam, without any intermediate diesel era, had already begun. The Shenfield electrics were of LNER design, far more modern than the Southern-inspired (if that is the term) designs that BR favoured in the 1950s, which were basically an assembly of hinged opening doors. This design had been good enough in Victorian times so why change a proven system? The LNER trains had guard-controlled sliding doors and belonged to a different era altogether. To compensate for this rash move into the mid-20th century, Liverpool Street itself was a wonderfully archaic, rabbit warren of a place, having grown piecemeal and uncontrolled. It had even proved necessary

to construct a footbridge connecting two sections of the station, which would otherwise have been inaccessible other than by venturing outside and re-entering by the back door, so to speak, on account of tracks barring the way to pedestrians.

But the station had considerable appeal to the art student, such as myself, who was looking for something with character, a bit out of the ordinary, and I spent several happy hours in a rather shabby refreshment room hardly changed from Great Eastern days. It was swept away in the great rebuilding and few mourned its passing. Not so when Euston was rebuilt in 1961/62 and the Great Hall removed, together with the magnificent Doric arch. I drew the accompanying picture there, with the statue of George Stephenson peering down on mere mortals. Not even John Betjeman could save it, although his efforts ensured that other threatened

examples of great Victorian architecture, notably St Pancras, would not suffer the same fate.

Below: **LIVERPOOL STREET** 1959 was the last full year of the Great Eastern Railway-designed, rebuilt 'B12' 4-6-0s. Two years earlier No 61550 is about to depart with a Southend train. One example, No 61572, survived until 1961, and has been preserved.

Above: **LIVERPOOL STREET** Among the earliest production main-line diesels were the English Electric 1Co-Co1s, the first of which entered service in 1958. Nos D200 and D202-5 were sent for trial on the Great Eastern section, and No D203 is seen at Liverpool Street on 3 February 1959 at the head of a Norwich express. 'B1' No 61001, the second-built of Thompson's very successful class of mixed-traffic 4-6-0s, dating from 1942, is waiting to take out a later Cambridge train. The EE Type 4s, later named Class 40, were very heavy, impressive-looking machines and did much of the pioneer diesel traction long-distance work on the East and West Coast routes, as well as the Great Eastern, but were soon superseded by later designs.

LIVERPOOL STREET Unlike at King's Cross, 'Pacifics' had never been allowed to venture within Liverpool Street's portals, not least on account of weight restrictions on the former Great Eastern lines in East Anglia. However, Bulleid 'light Pacifics' were tried out, with reasonable success, in the early days of nationalisation, so a batch of the first BR Standard 4-6-2s, the 'Britannias', were allocated to the Great Eastern section and proved very popular with crews and passengers, enabling substantial speeding up of the busy Ipswich and Norwich expresses. Here No 70000 *Britannia* herself leaves Liverpool Street with the 6.40pm train to Great Yarmouth.

Hitch-hiking to Scotland and back

1959 saw me heading north, hitching-hiking to Scotland. I'd regularly hitch-hiked during National Service and as an impecunious student it seemed the logical thing to carry on doing it. One hardly ever sees hitch-hikers today, but back then it was an everyday practice and over the years I travelled in just about everything from a motorcycle combination through various types of lorries to one memorable day on the A25 in a Rolls-Royce.

By the first day I had reached Leeds, hoping that I might meet up with the former London Transport 'Feltham' trams, very nearly my favourite mode of transport. These magnificent ground-breaking trams used to pass the top of our road in Thornton Heath, which meant that I got to travel on them regularly, and it was a sad day when they migrated to Leeds in 1950/51. I was out of luck, Leeds having just abandoned all its trams – current information in those days was difficult to come by, especially as one was an impecunious student.

But never mind – the railway scene opened new vistas for I was now in former North Eastern Railway territory. That was one of the truly great pre-Grouping companies, but living down south it seemed remote and epitomised the industrial north. I came across an old GNR 0-6-0 in Leeds, but then met NER 'B16' 4-6-0s and 0-8-0s, all very long-lived designs that would last into the 1960s, the 0-8-0s in particular – so long that two of them got themselves preserved.

NEVILLE HILL A North Eastern Railway 'Q6' 0-8-0 at Neville Hill shed, Leeds. In the background are a former LMS Fairburn 2-6-4T, a Stanier Class 5 4-6-0, and on 08 diesel shunter.

THIRSK No 61473, one of the highly regarded and long-lived Raven-designed NER 'B16/1' three-cylinder mixed-traffic 4-6-0s of 1920, heads a southbound freight.

DONCASTER Thompson rebuilt 17 of the Raven 4-6-0s in the mid-1940s with Walschaerts valve gear, being designated 'B1/3'. No 61464 is seen here at Doncaster with an down express, doing a very good impression of a Thompson 'B1' from this angle.

DONCASTER

my informant assured me. 'He used to drive like a madman and said he'd reached a dead end in his work, and everyone warned him but he took no notice and the inevitable happened.' He was not the only one of that astonishing generation who turned the contemporary painting world on its head, to die violently by their own hand.

Edinburgh was bathed in the early evening sunshine and I thought it the most beautiful city I had ever seen. I still do. There was plenty of steam about, although what would become the Class 26 and 27 diesel locomotives were already on the scene, as were Swindon-built Inter-City DMUs, on one of which I travelled next morning to Glasgow. 'Pacifics' were still much in evidence on both the East and West Coast routes, although local services were mostly in the hands of DMUs.

Below: **EDINBURGH WAVERLEY** 'D49' No 62729 departs eastwards with a train for North Berwick. In the adjacent platform is 'A3' No 60068 *Sir Visto* with a Waverley route train.

Above: **SELBY** No 60539 *Bronzino*, one of Peppercorn's handsome 'A2' 'Pacifics' of 1947, speeds through Selby with a northbound express. Nominally the most powerful of all British 'Pacifics', one, No 532 *Blue Peter*, has been preserved.

I arrived in Edinburgh courtesy of a lift from an American college lecturer who was able to enlighten me on the art scene across the water, which had just exploded on the UK art world – I would write my thesis on Modern Americans. Jackson Pollock in particular, with his huge 'action paintings', great exhilarating sweepings of colour flung at the canvas, had become, after some 20 years of relative obscurity, the most talked about of all the new wave, almost a household name. He had died three years earlier, in a car crash. 'Killed himself,'

EDINBURGH WAVERLEY 'J37' 0-6-0 No 64611 of North British origin pulls out with the 5.18pm stopping train to Corstorphine (I wonder why it was composed of corridor stock, mostly newish BR Mark 1s). Waiting to depart is an Aberdeen express in the charge of two Birmingham Sulzer Type 2 Bo-Bos (later Class 26).

Below: **ARGYLE STREET, GLASGOW** I had missed out on the trams in Leeds, but Glasgow still had a wonderful selection, some dating way back to the early days of the century, while at the other extreme were the handsome, streamlined post-war 'Cunarders', which, I had to admit, could give the 'Felthams' a run for their money. Here Glasgow ladies disembark from a 'Kilmarnock Bogie' of 1927-29 on a rather wet August morning. Alongside is a splendid Austin Sheerline limousine. In the distance is the bridge carrying Glasgow Central station over Argyle Street, and a post-war 'Cunarder' tram.

Right: **GLASGOW ST ENOCH** The neat-looking LMS-built 2P 4-4-0s, exemplified here by No 40621, were basically a Midland Railway design, and were multiplied after the Grouping. Not exactly the most powerful of passenger engines, they were said to be the most economical in the UK, something that appealed greatly to the cash-strapped LMS in the 1920s. St Enoch, built by the Glasgow & South Western Railway, no longer exists.

SOUTHPORT
The ex-Lancashire & Yorkshire Railway depot supplied motive power for trains to Preston and Manchester, and the Southport carriages to and from Euston, which were attached and detached from the main London to Liverpool train at Edge Hill. Present are Fairburn 2-6-4Ts Nos 42078 and 42132 with a Caprotti 5MT 4-6-0 just visible.

Above: **GLASGOW CENTRAL** Caledonian Railway-designed 0-4-4T No 55189 goes about its business at Glasgow Central. This particular locomotive was saved from breaking up by the Scottish Railway Preservation Society, and can be seen at Bowness beside the Firth of Forth.

Right: **SOUTHPORT** Stopping off on my way south, I made for Southport, a Lancashire resort with a beach that at high tide is wide enough for the world land speed record to have been recorded there in the 1920s. When I lived there in later years, I once saw an almost new E Type Jaguar with its interior being hosed down at my local garage one morning. 'Some idiot parked it on the beach last night, fell asleep, and just managed to climb out before the water washed him away. The car's a write off,' I was told. If 'the idiot' had been in one of these unique, converted ex-WD Bedford lorries he would have been fine, for they were specially adapted to carry visitors along the beach and out into the water – despite the somewhat apprehensive looks of some of the passengers.

SOUTHPORT A Fowler-designed 2-6-4T climbs away from Southport with a returning Wigan Wallgate excursion.

LIVERPOOL EXCHANGE
The busiest route out of Southport was that to Liverpool Exchange, which had been electrified by the Lancashire & Yorkshire Railway way back before the First World War, However, that didn't prevent some deranged senior official in the mid-1960s, based probably far away at BR headquarters at Marylebone or, most likely, Mars, from proposing its closure. The Southport to Preston line did close in 1964, but admittedly was not very well patronised. One of the handsome, if rather rough-riding, sliding-door EMUs built by the LMS in 1939 is seen in later years departing from Liverpool Exchange for Southport Chapel Street.

LIVERPOOL LIME STREET
The driver of Stanier 'Pacific' No 46250 *City of Lichfield* gets down to make some last-minute checks before setting off on the steep climb through the tunnels leading to Edge Hill and then hi-ho for London.

Being lucky enough (ha-ha) to be invited to join Her Majesty's Royal Air Force, I was sent to RAF West Kirby in January 1956, having spent my very first week kitting out at RAF Cardington in the great airship sheds built there for the ill-fated R101. We travelled from there to West Kirby, on the Cheshire Lines Committee route that closed in May 1962, behind a Midland Compound 4-4-0. The allowance of a weekend pass home halfway through my eight weeks at West Kirby did afford me the opportunity to travel behind both 'Princess Royal' and 'Princess Coronation' 'Pacifics', though I wouldn't claim that this was adequate compensation for suffering the tender mercies of bullying corporal drill instructors!

SANDHILLS The complex of lines in the Liverpool dock area is typified by this picture of a Stanier 5MT 4-6-0 accelerating through Sandhills with the morning Liverpool Exchange to Glasgow express. Before 1923 the Lancashire & Yorkshire and the London & North Western railways were rivals for the Merseyside to Scotland traffic out of Exchange and Lime Street stations respectively. This traffic continued after amalgamation and, indeed, until the end of steam and the eventual closure of Exchange, except for the underground station there. Sandhills was the junction for the lines from Exchange to Aintree, Preston and beyond, and Southport.

WATFORD TUNNEL Rebuilt 'Royal Scot' 4-6-0 No 46158 approaches the tunnel with a Liverpool to Euston express. The West Coast route had nothing like the number of 'Pacifics' that the East Coast route could boast, and therefore the highly capable rebuilt 'Scots' handled many of the top-link duties.

Ireland

With money earned from my holiday employment I decided to visit Ireland in September 1959. The troubled relationship between England and Ireland, and the Celtic culture, were two draws that took me across the water, as also was the fact that, although dieselisation was greatly advanced in the Republic, there were still pockets of steam. Had I owned a crystal ball I would have been utterly delighted to discover that I would meet the beautiful Maeve, a student at University College, Dublin (and *not* named after Ireland's most famous steam locomotive!) while she was working as a waitress in a hotel on the seafront at Eastbourne in 1967 and get married in Dublin the following year.

OLD OAK COMMON No 4075 *Cardiff Castle*, the third member of that illustrious class of GWR express locomotives built between 1923 and 1950, speeds past Old Oak Common with a Fishguard boat train.

Right: **WATERFORD** Having crossed at night from Fishguard I arrived at Rosslare early the following morning to find that a rather grubby Metropolitan-Vickers Co-Co diesel had charge of the boat train that conveyed me to Waterford. There I was delighted to come upon No 157, one of the legendary 'J15' or '101' Class 0-6-0s. There were 119 in all, originating in 1867, the last survivor not being withdrawn until 99 years later, an extraordinary record. No 157 is leaving with the 10.40am to Wexford via New Ross, its single carriage a Great Southern & Western Railway clerestory dating from the early 1900s. Two years later I would ride this route again behind a 'J15' a few days before the line shut to passenger traffic. Two 'J15s' have been preserved.

Below: **CORK** was a wonderful time-warp in 1959, and a very attractive city; I went to see *South Pacific* in the big cinema in the city centre. The overnight goods for Dublin curves around the passenger station at Cork before it accelerates through the tunnel and up the fierce gradient facing departing trains. The locomotive is No 402, one of the big Watson-designed express passenger 4-6-0s of 1916-23. Watson had come from Swindon and was clearly influenced by the 'Star' Class. But his four-cylinder locomotives were little short of disastrous. Despite the Great Southern Railway, into which most Irish railway companies within independent Eire were amalgamated in 1925, being in dire financial straits, it scrapped three of the '400s' in 1929/30. The rest were rebuilt with two cylinders, No 402 being the first in 1927, resulting in a halfway decent design that lasted until dieselisation. By 1959 passenger services between Dublin and Cork had been totally dieselised but No 402 was one of the last two survivors of the class, by now confined to freight work, being withdrawn in 1961. A 'J15' is shunting cattle trucks in the background – moving cattle was still big business in 1959.

CORK Despite dieselisation, there was a fine selection of steam locomotives on the shed at Cork. Among the group seen here are a 'J15' and two 'J26' 0-6-0Ts of M&GWR origin; there were 12 members of the latter class, the only reasonably large number of this wheel arrangement in Ireland, which was so common on the opposite side of the water. There is also a Woolwich 2-6-0, of a Maunsell SE&CR design bought after the end of the 1914-18 war, and one of the unique Cork, Bandon & South Coast Railway Beyer Peacock 4-6-0Ts.

1959 Happenings (4)

December

- First episode of children's animated TV programme *Ivor the Engine*, made by Oliver Postgate and Peter Firmin's Smallfilms
- In first Cold War arms control treaty, 12 countries, including USA and USSR, agree to set aside Antarctica as scientific preserve and ban military activity there
- Makarios III selected as first President of independent Cyprus

Below left: **CORK** The first three carriages in this rake of ancient wooden-bodied specimens, used at weekends for trips to the seaside at Youghal, are six-wheelers of GS&WR and Midland & Great Western Railway origin. These were the only six-wheelers I can ever recall seeing still at work in either the UK or Ireland.

Below right: **GALWAY** Moving on to Galway I came across yet another 'first', the one and only chance I ever got to photograph a 2-4-0 at work. This wheel arrangement went back into the mists of time, but the 20 members of this class of former Midland & Great Western locomotives were relatively modern, dating from 1893-98. They held their own against the 4-4-0s that succeeded them, and No 652, seen shunting in the goods yard beside the sea at Galway, was the last survivor of the class, being withdrawn in 1963.

DUBLIN AMIENS STREET The Great Northern Railway of Ireland retained its separate identity until it went bankrupt in September 1958, when it was divided between CIE in the Republic and the Ulster Transport Authority in Northern Ireland. Most of its passenger services were in the hands of a succession of 4-4-0s, nearly all of them excellent. 'U' Class No 197 *Lough Neagh*, dating from 1915 (although five more were built as late as 1948, again by Beyer Peacock in Manchester) arrives at Amiens Street with a stopping train from Drogheda. It retains its gorgeous lined blue GNR livery and is commendably clean, the only indication that the GNR has ceased to exist being its new owner's initials stencilled on the buffer beam.

LLANDUDNO JUNCTION I returned home by way of Dun Laoghaire and Holyhead. The most important junction on the North Wales coast was Llandudno Junction, and in this 1959 picture the sidings are packed with carriages, almost all of them of LMS origin, while LMS-designed 5MT 4-6-0s abound.

France

December 1959 I made my first trip abroad – I've never been quite able to think of Ireland as a foreign country. My fellow art student, Harry Isles, had worked at a café, Maurice's, on the West Bank in Paris in the summer of 1959, and said that Maurice would put us up for a few days around the New Year. Being in straitened financial circumstances, as always, once across the Channel at Calais

We attempted to hitch-hike to Paris, but got no further than Boulogne. As darkness fell we decided we could just about afford the train fare. Making our way to Tintilleries station, we booked return tickets – well, it sort of guaranteed that we'd get back home even if we starved during our stay – and shortly a big, dark green 'Pacific' wreathed in steam emerged out of the darkness, we climbed several steps from the low platform into a dark green carriage, and we were off. Everything reeked of abroad: the layout, the appointments, the upholstery, and the notices in four languages forbidding the hurling of objects out of the window, which we discovered we could lower right down and climb out of – not that we did. It was wonderful.

This really was abroad as I had imagined it. Paris was, of course, well, Paris and, with its Traction Avant Citroen taxis and those wonderful, futuristic-looking DS Citroens in the showrooms on the Champs Élysées, tall, almost prehistoric-looking open-back buses, barges on the Seine in front of Notre Dame, where 13 years later on Christmas Day 1972 we would give our seven-month-old son William his bottle during mass, a bouncing electric train that took us to Versailles, and the glorious architecture, it was all that I had hoped. We managed to make alcoholic and non-alcoholic drinks last almost indefinitely while sitting in outdoor cafes around the city and down in the Metro would be following

Left: **BOULOGNE** SNCF 141R 2-8-2 heads a train from Lille. The 141Rs were amongst the finest steam engines ever built. Constructed in the USA and Canada, all 1,340 were delivered in a remarkably short period, between November 1945 and September 1947, and played the major part in reviving the French railway system after the devastations of the Second World War. They worked just about everywhere in France, being capable of hauling every type of train from passenger expresses to heavy freight. I travelled behind a 141R more than once on boat trains between Amiens and Boulogne and Calais, and examples remained until the very end of French steam on 17 October 1975. Twelve have been preserved.

Above: **PARIS GARE DU NORD** When we arrived at the Gare du Nord we felt that we had entered a Monet painting, with purple and yellow-tinted steam and smoke rising high into the roof. One of the Chapelon-designed 231K 'Pacifics', originally designed for the Etat Railway, waits at the head of a boat train for Calais.

PARIS METRO One of the original Metro units near Pigalle.

PARIS GARE DU NORD SNCF 2-8-2T No 141TC15 sets out with a suburban train. This wheel arrangement, the equivalent of our 2-6-4T and 2-6-2T, was much favoured around Paris. Seventy of these handsome tank engines were built by the Nord Railway in 1932-35, just before it was absorbed by SNCF, and were a familiar sight to visitors arriving in Paris from the Channel ports until the withdrawal of the last members of the class in 1970.

in the footsteps of Toulouse Lautrec, Degas, etc, was misplaced. Most of it was pretty run-of-the-mill, just like in London. We travelled a lot on the Metro, by way of some of its marvellous Art Nouveau stations. It was cheap and not much like the London Underground. The carriages were short and, while just as bouncy and rattly as London ones, had a very distinctive smell, of which garlic formed a large part. All but some vastly more modern ones, which ran on rubber tyres, were ancient. The First Class cars were painted red, the rest green.

PARIS In this 1968 view, the Renault TN6 bus dates from the early 1930s, while among the cars in the background is a brand-new DS Citroen, much in evidence during my visit in 1959.

Index